Books Without Borders

Reaching Global Readers with AI Translation

C.M. Bilson

Shenanigans Press

For permission requests, please contact:

Shenanigans Press

PO Box 323, MORAYFIELD QLD 4506 AUSTRALIA

Email: cait@caitlynlynch.com

Contents

ADVISORY NOTE

All information in this book was believed to be correct and current at the time of publication (July 2025). However, publishing guidelines, platform policies, and legal requirements are subject to change. Please verify critical details for your own situation before acting.

Nothing in this book should be constituted as legal advice. For legal or business decisions, always consult a qualified professional or the relevant authorities in your jurisdiction.

Introduction: Why Translate?

My Journey as an Indie Author

I've been writing for as long as I can remember… or, if you ask my mother, even longer. She claims that almost as soon as she taught me to read, I started scribbling my own stories. I was never satisfied with the endings of the books I devoured as a child, so I would sit down with a pencil and paper and continue the story until I was happy, even if that meant writing a hundred extra pages.

My first brush with publishing, however, was a disaster. In my early twenties, I wrote my first original novel, a horribly derivative fantasy. Naïvely, I started querying agents and publishers, desperate for a foot in the door. Instead, I fell for the polished promises of a vanity press. In 2000, I paid them £1,200 (I was living in the UK then) and my one and only royalty cheque was for just 67 pence.

It was a hard lesson, and it soured me on the publishing world for a long time. I kept writing, but only for myself. Then, pretty much by accident, I stumbled onto online fanfic forums. Tentatively, I posted a few stories and braced myself for feedback. The enthusiastic response spurred me on.

Fanfiction became my training ground. Over the next decade, I wrote around three million words of fanfic, entirely for free. I ran a "birthdays blog," gifting 1,000-word stories in my fandom to anyone who asked. Writing to order on a deadline taught me how to write fast and how to hit the emotional beats readers craved. The real-time feedback on my episodic stories was a masterclass in writing to market, and pivoting quickly if the latest chapter didn't get the reception I'd expected.

It was my fanfic readers who gave me the final push. They urged me to try original romance, insisting that I deserved to get paid for my words. In 2014, I finally took the plunge into indie publishing, putting my first book up on Amazon. To my astonishment, it sold well and continues to sell even now.

Back then, I was juggling two young kids, and life threw another curveball when my husband developed a debilitating and permanent back injury. Suddenly, I had no other choice but to become the family breadwinner. Writing had to fit into the cracks of busy days and late nights, but I kept going. Over the years, I built a backlist of over fifty books. Some were short, some long, some commercial successes, others less so. Marketing and social media were never my strengths, but by stubborn persistence I slowly grew my income to the point where I was making low four figures most months.

And then I heard about ScribeShadow.

***

Expanding Markets – and Running Into Roadblocks

I've always been eager to connect with new readers, but during the pandemic, I discovered an entirely new way to reach audiences: audio narration. I started out narrating a few of my own books, mostly out of curiosity to see if I could, but I do have amateur acting experience and a voice and accent that sound as though I escaped from an Austen adaptation, tailor-made for narrating Regency romances. Before long, I was narrating not just my own books but taking on projects for other authors as well. What began as an experiment soon grew into a professional second career. Bringing stories to life through audio opened up a brand-new audience and significantly increased my revenue streams.

That success made me wonder: if audio could expand my reach, what about translation? I began researching the possibilities, imagining my stories in the hands of readers all over the world. But the reality was sobering. Quotes for translating just my most popular four-book series into German averaged over 10,000 Euros, an eye-watering amount when converted to the Australian dollars I was earning. For me, it simply wasn't an option. I was struggling to make my mortgage payments many months.

I didn't give up on the idea, but I set it aside for a while. The dream of seeing my books in other languages never really faded. When I heard about ScribeShadow, a tool that promised quality translation at a fraction of the usual cost, I was sceptical but curious. I ran the numbers, and realized that, for less than the cost of one book translated to one language using the traditional methods, I could translate *my entire backlist* into half a dozen languages.

For the first time, expanding into new markets felt possible. The barrier that had always seemed insurmountable started to crumble, replaced by a sense of real, actionable opportunity. Instead of picking just one book or one language, I could open the door to readers in Germany, France, Italy, and beyond. ScribeShadow made that a reality.

The Elephant in the Room: The Ethics of Using AI to Translate

Am I taking the job of an actual translator?

Well, no. The reality is, I could never have afforded to hire one in the first place. When I started exploring translation, the professional translators I contacted were all booked out for months. The quotes I received were far beyond what I could manage as an indie author. And all those translators are still working, primarily for traditional publishers, who can pay their rates and wait for their timelines.

Over the last year or so since I started using AI translation, I've had honest conversations with several translators. Many admitted they'd been using AI as an assistive tool long before authors like me even heard about it (DeepL, which I'll discuss in the next chapter, has been around since 2017). For some, it's a way to speed up their process and take on more work. For others, it's a tool they choose not to use, and that's their choice. Some have shifted their focus to editing AI-produced translations and are busier than ever, working as quality control and language experts.

For many indie authors like me, the alternative to AI-assisted translation isn't a human translator; it's **no translation at all**. Without AI, my books would remain accessible only to English-speaking readers. Using these new tools isn't about undercutting professionals. It's about making it possible to reach readers I otherwise never could have, and doing so in a way that's sustainable for an indie career.

I believe translation is transformative, not generative. The story is mine, the *ideas* are mine, and the technology is just a bridge that helps it cross into a new language. Without AI, I wouldn't be able to cross over at all.

We're all using AI, whether you want to acknowledge it or not. If you drive a modern car, use a washing machine, use Google to do research, talk to Siri or Alexa, or even rely on predictive text, you're using AI. How much you choose to use it is up to you. Personally, I choose to use AI for the things I am not good at. I don't need it to plot or write my stories. But it makes a good marketing assistant and an excellent translator, and that's the usage level I'm currently comfortable with.

There's a Douglas Adams quote I find very pertinent to

the whole AI situation at the present time, and you might relate to it as well:

> *"I've come up with a set of rules that describe our reactions to technologies:*
> *1. Anything that is in the world when you're born is normal and ordinary and is just a natural part of the way the world works.*
> *2. Anything that's invented between when you're fifteen and thirty-five is new and exciting and revolutionary and you can probably get a career in it.*
> *3. Anything invented after you're thirty-five is against the natural order of things."*
> **Douglas Adams,** The Salmon of Doubt: Hitchhiking the Galaxy One Last Time

But What About Trolls?

Ugh, trolls. Keyboard warriors. Yes, there may well be people who target you for using AI to translate. Honestly, I liken them to militant vegans... let me explain that analogy.

I'm an animal lover. My cats are rescues, I volunteer regularly at a local rescue centre, and a good, heart-wrenching animal story is the fastest way to bring me to tears. But I did grow up on a farm, and I am not a vegetarian. I accept that this is a contradiction in my personal ethical framework, and I have the deepest respect for vegetarians and vegans who make their choices out of a stronger sense of ethics than I have. More power to them.

BUT.

Imagine a militant vegan who makes a point of walking into every burger joint they came across, marching up to people trying to quietly eat their meals, and screaming "MEAT IS MURDER!" in their faces.

That's how the militantly anti-AI people are coming across right now.

Yes, we know AI usage may not be the most ethical thing out there. We know it may not be brilliant for the planet.

It would be naïve to pretend there aren't ethical grey areas when it comes to using AI for translation, or creative work of any kind. The questions can be uncomfortable: How was the AI model trained? Did it use copyrighted works without permission? Does it consume power and water at non-environmentally friendly rates?

These concerns are real, and they're important to acknowledge. The technology is evolving so quickly that laws, industry standards, and even our sense of what's "fair" or "right" are struggling to keep up. The grey areas will continue to challenge us, but acknowledging them is the first step to navigating them thoughtfully.

Right now, however, these tools are perfectly legal to use, if you access them in a legal manner.

It is legal to use this transformative technology to translate the words YOU have written into other languages, and to sell them on major platforms around the world. You're not a criminal if you choose to do it, and don't let anyone try to tell you that you are.

We're just trying to survive in an increasingly technological world that's changing at absolutely dizzying speed. And AIs aren't going away.

In the end, technology is just a tool, and tools can be used wisely or carelessly. As indie authors, we are used to wearing many hats and finding creative solutions to challenges that once would have stopped us cold. AI translation, for all its complications, is another tool that lets us reach readers in places we never could have dreamed of.

> You are allowed to use the resources available to you. You are allowed to experiment, to learn, and to grow. Using AI doesn't make you less of an author, and it doesn't mean you value books or writing any less. In fact, it shows you care enough to put your story into the hands of readers who might otherwise never get to read it.

Don't let fear, or the loud voices online, stop you from sharing your work. Make informed choices, act with integrity, and keep your focus on your readers. It's your story, and you have every right to tell it in as many languages as you can.

Take another look at that Douglas Adams quote. And make your decisions based on your own code of ethics, and what's best for your business (because if you're not treating your writing as a business, why are you even reading this book?).

The Landscape: Translating in the AI Era

Traditional Translation vs. AI Translation: Pros and Cons

When most authors imagine their book in another language, they picture a skilled professional poring over every sentence, finding just the right turn of phrase. Traditional translation has long been considered the gold standard; thorough, nuanced, and, when done well, nearly invisible to the reader.

But here's the truth: even the most careful human translation is not immune to criticism. If you want proof, go to the German or French Amazon sites and look up your favourite big-name, traditionally published author. Scroll through the reviews, and look at the low-star ones. Chances are, you'll see readers taking issue with the translation, sometimes harshly. They might call out clunky dialogue, awkward cultural references, or a lack of the author's original "voice." And these are definitely not machine translations, but the result of expensive, professional work.

The same goes for AI translation. Reviewers can and will be just as unforgiving if the translation does not feel natural or true to the story. The reality is, there's no way to guarantee a "perfect" translation, no matter which approach you choose. Both methods have their strengths and weaknesses, and both are subject to the tastes and expectations of readers in the target language.

Traditional translation is often slower and much more expensive, but it brings a human touch and cultural understanding that technology is only beginning to approach. **AI translation** is fast, affordable, and accessible to indie authors, but still requires careful review and often benefits from human editing or feedback.

In the end, there is no real "win." Every translation, whether produced by a human or a machine, will be judged on its own merits by readers who have their own opinions and preferences. The important thing is to approach the process thoughtfully, stay open to feedback, and remember that connecting with new readers is always worth the effort.

Why Many Indie Authors Haven't Tried Translation Yet

For most indie authors, translation feels out of reach.

The biggest hurdle is simple: cost. Getting even a single book translated by a professional can run into thousands of dollars or euros. If you have a series, those expenses multiply quickly. For a lot of us, that is just not feasible, especially when there is no guarantee those translated editions will earn back the investment.

Even traditional publishers are often hesitant. They will only pay for translations if the book proves itself in English, but they might still hold tightly to the rights.

> If you are traditionally published, read your contract carefully. You may be able to ask for a rights reversion in certain languages if the publisher has not exercised those rights within a set timeframe.

Time is another factor. Even if you can afford it, traditional translation is slow. You might be waiting months or longer for your book to be available in another language. That is a long time to wait for a potential return, especially in a fast-moving indie market.

Then there is the fear of the unknown. Most indie authors do not speak the languages they would like to translate into. That makes the process feel risky. How do you judge the quality of a translation you cannot read? How do you market to readers in another country, or handle customer service questions in a language you do not know? It can all feel overwhelming.

There is also the perception that translation is only for the "big names," that you need to be a bestseller before it's even worth considering. Many authors worry about negative reviews, or about putting out a product that is not up to their usual standards, especially if they cannot personally check the work.

Finally, the tools themselves have, until recently, been clunky or hard to access. The idea of using AI for translation is still new, and many authors simply do not know where to start or which services to trust.

All these factors combine to make translation feel like a risk, rather than an opportunity. But the landscape is changing fast, and those barriers are starting to come down.

Overview of Current AI Translation Tools

Not long ago, most indie authors assumed translation meant either a huge professional expense or using clunky, unreliable machine tools that delivered a poor reader experience. That landscape is changing rapidly, thanks to a new wave of AI-powered solutions designed to bring translation within reach for authors at every level.

ScribeShadow is a standout among these tools, and for good reason. It was written, and is actively maintained, by a professional software engineer who is also an indie romance author. This unique combination means ScribeShadow was built from the ground up for *fiction*, not non-fiction or business documents. Unlike most general-purpose translation tools, its algorithm has been trained to understand the challenges of storytelling, character voice, and dialogue. It's particularly strong at handling colloquialisms and localizing language for specific markets, so jokes, slang, and cultural references don't get lost or sound awkward in translation.

Of course, ScribeShadow is not the only tool out there, but it is the only one (so far) that takes the specific needs of fiction authors seriously. Here are a few other options:

- **DeepL** is widely regarded as producing more natural-sounding translations than Google Translate, especially for European languages, and it translates to a vast number of languages. It's been around for a long time, too, first launching in 2017, well before the large-language models (LLMs) that we currently recognise as 'AI' existed. However, it's important to know what DeepL was originally designed for: technical documents, business correspondence, and non-fiction materials. Its algorithms excel at translating precise language, instructions, and terminology. While it can create readable translations for fiction, it often lacks sensitivity to character voice, emotional nuance, and creative dialogue. You may find that DeepL handles a business report beautifully, but struggles with a witty banter between characters or cultural slang that needs careful adaptation for a new audience.

- **Google Translate** is fast and free, supporting dozens of languages, but it tends to struggle the most with dialogue, idioms, and character voice. I use it for when I need a quick-and-dirty translation of another language back to English so I can get the gist – of a comment on a Facebook post, for example, of to figure out what categories I want to use in the German Amazon store.

- **Babelcube** connects authors with human translators and works on a royalty-share basis. While not AI-based, it's an option if you want human translation without upfront payment, though quality and timelines can vary widely. *(I have one translation with Babelcube, a short novella in Portuguese. It's been available for several years and has never reached the payment threshold to actually pay me. The payment threshold... of $10.)*

- **Microsoft Translator** and other machine translation tools are useful for short texts or web content, but aren't optimized for full-length fiction.

- **ChatGPT, Claude, Gemini and other large-language AI models**: at its core, ScribeShadow uses these models, and you can too. But it may take a lot of time, effort and tweaking your prompts in order to get those benefits of the AI understanding exactly HOW you want your work translated and to match the correct tone for your fiction. If you want to use it for other languages that aren't currently available through ScribeShadow, you could always give it a go! I have plans to attempt to use DeepL for a basic translation and then ChatGPT or Claude to edit, but the sheer amount of time I know it's going to take is making me hesitate.

It's worth noting that ScribeShadow does have limitations. At the moment, it's only available in about a dozen languages, and several of those are still in beta. This means the translation quality may vary depending on the language you choose, and not every market is covered yet. If you write in a genre that's popular in a language not yet supported, you may need to wait for future updates or look to other tools in the meantime. As the software develops, more languages and refinements are likely, but for now, your options are somewhat limited to the supported list.

No tool, even ScribeShadow, is entirely "set and forget." AI translation is getting better every month, but you'll still want to review the results and, if possible, get feedback from speakers of your target language. What matters most is that, for the first time, indie fiction authors have a translation tool available to us that actually understands the craft (and the quirks) of storytelling.

BEFORE YOU TRANSLATE: THINGS I WISH I'D KNOWN

Start With Your Bestselling Book, and Ideally, a Series

This is the number one thing I wish someone had told me. When I first tried this process, I tentatively dipped my toe in with a short novella that had never sold well in English. Unsurprisingly, it did not sell very well in French or German either. (Spoiler: translation does not magically turn a slow seller into a bestseller.)

That said, the translation paid for itself without advertising and did well enough to encourage me to keep going. The real growth happened when I translated a four-book series that had already proven itself with English readers. If you are going to invest time, energy, or money, start with the book or series starter that is already your strongest performer.

Success in translation almost always starts with success at home.

What Language Should I Do First?

A question I get asked all the time is: *Which language should I start with?* My answer depends on your marketing strategy. The recommendations below also assume you are planning to sell your ebook in Kindle Unlimited in all these markets (except Dutch, where KU doesn't exist, and you'll have to be wide). I do not yet have a lot of experience wide, though I am putting in some Dutch titles and starting to move some underperforming KU titles wide to experiment. If you are already doing well with direct sales or on Kobo or Google Play, you will probably be able to figure it out with translated books too.

If you spend money on ads:

1. French
2. Italian
3. German
4. Spanish
5. Brazilian Portuguese
6. Dutch

If you do not have money to spend on ads:

1. French
2. German
3. Italian
4. Spanish

Why this order?

French and German markets offer surprisingly good organic discovery for indie books. Readers in these countries actually stumble across new books on their own, even without paid advertising. Italy and Spain can be fantastic if you are running Facebook ads. The price per click can be staggeringly low compared to the US market. Sometimes it feels like advertising costs are from a different decade.

Brazil can be a tough nut to crack because in my experience, there is pretty much zero organic discovery. Unless you advertise, you won't sell. Brazilians rarely purchase ebooks, but they do binge-read in KU. The per-page-read payout is only about 30 percent of the US KENP rate. Unless you speak the language or have family connections in Brazil, it might not be your best first choice.

But ScribeShadow Has Other Languages...

I know. I am currently experimenting in Dutch. There is anecdotal evidence that Kobo Plus offers great returns for Dutch translations. I don't have a ton of experience wide, but it does seem that free first-in-series is the way to go... which means that, once again, SERIES of books are what you need to get this to work.

Bottom line:
Start with the market that matches your strengths. If you have an ad budget, experiment with France or Italy. If you rely on organic sales, try French or German. Do not feel pressured to go everywhere at once. Pick one, learn the ropes, and build from there.

Should I Do All My Backlist Books in One Language Before Moving On to the Next?

This is another thing I wish someone had told me at the beginning.

***Yes*, you absolutely should.**

The reason is simple: it's extremely confusing to work in multiple languages at once. For every book you translate, you will need to translate not just the book itself, but also the blurb, keywords, and, if you are advertising, tag lines and ad copy. You will need to format every book to add a copyright section. (More on the specific requirements for European markets later.) You also need to update your About the Author or More Books by the Author page.

It is much easier to do all of this at once for a batch of books in German, for example, than to do one in German, one in French, and one in Spanish. If you do not speak all these languages, it's very easy to accidentally put your Spanish copyright page in your Italian translation.

(Why no, I've never done that. What makes you ask?

Okay, yes, I totally did that and it was embarrassing. I made the mistake so you don't have to.)

Once you have your backlist up in all the languages you want to work in, and you are moving on to frontlist and future releases, you will hopefully have built a good workflow for each language. You will start to recognize your commonly used phrases and have templates for things like the copyright page, making things much less confusing.

Publish Paperback Editions

Europeans love paperbacks. Twelve percent of my income in France is from paperback sales, and it's not much less in Germany. Italy and Spain also have decent paperback sales, a higher percentage than the US for sure. Talk to your cover artist about a "bulk deal" to get all the text redone on your covers and all the paperbacks made at once.

I started off only publishing through Amazon KDP Print, but I'm steadily expanding to also publish through Draft2Digital and Ingram Spark, because Amazon has much less of a monopoly in European countries.

Brazil is more complicated because Amazon don't print in Brazil and Ingram Spark at this stage have very limited distribution there. At this stage, I haven't bothered much with paperbacks for Brazilian books... though that's changing with a new opportunity that's recently presented. See the Paperback Distribution chapter for more info!

Step By Step with ScribeShadow

Before You Translate Anything

Before you upload your book and start translating, pause and think about your book's title in the target language. This is one of the most important steps, and it's often overlooked. That clever or punny title you love in English might become complete gibberish in

French, sound awkward in Italian, or even be accidentally offensive in German. Direct translations rarely capture the right feeling, and sometimes they give entirely the wrong impression.

But Do I Have to Translate My Title?

Some people don't. And especially if your cover artist isn't willing to play ball, it might be something to consider. I'd definitely translate the series title at least. Amazon does helpfully label books things like "German Edition" to reduce confusion.

HOWEVER.

Personally I find it a bit... disrespectful? Like I just couldn't be bothered? And if you are a social media maven with big plans to use TikTok or Instagram to promote your foreign editions, I can tell you that the number one question you'll get if you promote a book with an English-appearing title in Germany is "Is this available in German?" EVEN IF you are literally saying in the video or captions that it's a German edition.

The TL:DR for me is: YES. Yes, you should translate titles if it's possible for you to do so.

How I Choose Titles

Here is what I do. I start a conversation with ChatGPT, or you can use whatever AI LLM you prefer. I give the AI my book's title, blurb, and main tropes, and tell it which language I am targeting. I ask for title suggestions that are not necessarily direct translations, but that capture the book's vibe, genre, and appeal for readers in the target language. I want options that would make someone browsing in that language stop and look, not just a literal copy of my original, especially if an idiom doesn't translate well. If it's a series, I will give the information for the series title and all of the books up front and ask for suggestions for the entire series.

Once I have a list of possible titles, I go to the Amazon store for that country and search for those titles. I check to see if they are already in use, and what kinds of books come up, and yes, sometimes I go back to the drawing board and start again. Some of my book and series titles are VERY different in other languages.

A Note About German Titles:

Germany has a strict rule: you cannot use a title that is already in use. If your preferred title is taken, you can make it unique by adding a subtitle. I usually list the series title and book number as my subtitle, but you can also use a genre tag, such as "An epic sci-fi romance." This keeps your book discoverable and makes sure you follow the rules.

Blurbs

I like to go through a similar process for the blurb, giving ChatGPT my original and asking it to translate to the target language using the chosen book and series titles. You can translate blurbs in ScribeShadow, but you have to use credits for them. Doing them with AI chat is free. I often ask for suggested Amazon keywords or Facebook ad headlines in my target language to use as well.

Next Step: Uploading to ScribeShadow

Once you have settled on your title, it's time to get your manuscript ready for translation. ScribeShadow makes this part pretty straightforward, but there are a few things you can do ahead of time to make the process smoother.

Preparing Your Manuscript

- **Final version only.** Make sure you are uploading your finished, proofread manuscript. You cannot (at time of writing this guide) edit your book within the ScribeShadow interface. If you spot a mistake after uploading and before translating, you'll need to delete, fix, and reupload.

- **Keep formatting simple.** ScribeShadow does a great job with standard formatting like chapter breaks, italics, and scene breaks. If your file has fancy fonts, embedded images, or complicated tables, consider stripping those out or simplifying them. You should go back through the translation afterwards and check that it all looks how you want it to.

- **File type.** You can use either a .docx or a .epub. If you upload a docx, you can only download a docx.

If you upload an epub, you can choose to download an epub or a docx.

- What you choose will depend on how you plan to reformat the book afterwards, which you absolutely should do (I'll go into more detail about how and why in the next chapter). I personally use Atticus, and I've found the best results with uploading and downloading docx files. Epubs sometimes 'eat' scene breaks and going through to find them and put them back in the right place can be painful. Results may vary if you use Vellum, InDesign, Affinity or some other publishing software... but in my experience, simple is best, and docx files give consistently good results.

Uploading Your Book

Go to the ScribeShadow website (app.scribeshadow.com) and log in with your account. If you do not have an account yet, register first. You'll need to select a subscription plan.

I should probably note here that I'm not in any way employed by ScribeShadow. However, I do have an affiliate code which you can use if you wish. Here's the details on how that works, screenshot straight from the site. You'll get 50% off your first month; the highest tier this works with is the Bestseller US$199/month tier... so you can save US$99.50 by using this. Up to you; full transparency on the graphic of how it works and the benefit to me.

Yes, my code is OUXGECDR.

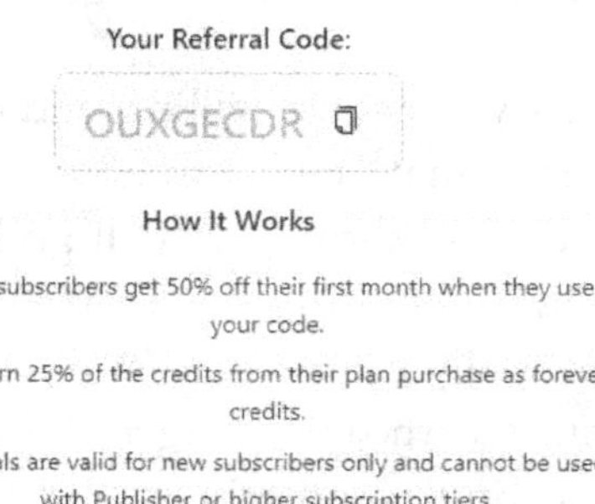

Upload your book, and enter the book title (in English), series title if you have one, and author name. ScribeShadow will create a page for your book. All translations of this book will now be managed from this page.

The Cost of Translations

For the regular languages (those not in beta) *approximately* 1 word to 1 language = 1 credit.*

So to translate a 30,000 word novella to French, you'll need to spend 30,000 credits. Consider the size of your backlist, how many books you want to translate into how many languages, and how fast you want to get translations out, and choose a monthly plan accordingly. You can cancel at any time and nothing happens to already-translated books. They just stay in your account.

If you do not have enough credits left in your monthly total to translate a whole book, you have some options:

- Unused credits carry forward for one month only – so if you have some unused credits in June, you need to use them by the end of July. Unused credits get used 'first' so as long as you're doing SOME translating each month, it's OK to carry forward a small balance.
- You can translate chapter by chapter to use them up and wait until next month to finish the book.
- You can "renew early," which restarts your subscription at the current date.
- You can buy some "forever credits," which never expire. I find it is handy to have a small stock of these. I will receive some if you use my affiliate code, for which I thank you!

*Sometimes, certain AI models may have a discounted rate. Certain languages may have a different rate... Hindi, in beta at time of writing, appears to use almost double the amount of credits.

All right. Let's get translating.

1. **Upload your book, if you didn't already. You can add the cover if you want, but it's not required.**

2. **Create your metadata in your original language:**

   Add genre, blurb, and some tropes and keywords. This information is provided to the AI in the prompt to translate and can influence choices the AI makes. For example, if you tell the AI your book is a middle grade novel, it will use different language than for adult readers.

3. **Create your metadata in the target language:**

   In the metadata page (after clicking on the book), click on the language dropdown box at the top and select Add Language. This is where you will put your translated title. I also recommend adding your translated blurb.

4. **Never Translate and Always Translate:**

   Let's say you've created something that's a clever acronym in English... like SHIELD, for example, for a government agency. It would be extremely difficult, if not impossible, to create an acronym in German which would also be similarly representative. This would be a case for Never Translate. Or let's say you have something you'd like to translate the same way every time... like a planet you've named Frost's Edge. There are several ways you could translate that into German. You might have a discussion with ChatGPT, work out which one you'd like, and enter this into Always Translate. Have a really good think about these before you start the translations. It's fiddly to fix them later.

5. **Remove anything you do not want to translate:**

   I strip out the table of contents, copyright page, and About the Author pages. These are the same across every book, so why waste credits to translate them every time? I'm all about economy. Atticus will build me a new table of contents, and I have master pages saved for copyright and About the Author in every language. I will put them back in when I reformat. If you're planning to use the epub straight from ScribeShadow to Amazon, however, leave all this in.

Translating Your Book

- **Select your target language:**

  Click on a chapter in the left-hand column (it does not matter which chapter if you are translating the whole book). Choose the language you want to translate into from the available list. Choose either "Translate Entire Book" or "Translate Chapter." ScribeShadow will tell you how many credits you are about to spend out of your available total.

- **Always translate from your original language:**

  You don't want to end up playing some weird game of Telephone. Try it out. Go and paste the opening few lines from any book into Google Translate and bounce through a dozen or so languages, then back to English. The result might be completely unrecognizable.

- **Select your AI model:**

  The developer behind ScribeShadow regularly evaluates new models and will incorporate them into the software if appropriate. There will always be one that is currently recommended.

- **If you write "steamy":**

  Some AI models are prudish. Some chapters may fail (you will not be charged credits if they do). You can retry, or check the AI model dropdown list and see if there is a different one recommended for steamy scenes.

- **If you are translating to German:**

  There are two different types of quotation marks for German: guillemets or German quotation marks. Guillemets are recommended, but you can choose the other style if you prefer.

- **Push the Translate button and wait for the book to process.**

It should only take a few minutes.

Next Steps: Proofing, Reformatting, and Back Matter

Proofreading

You have an option to proofread your translated book in ScribeShadow. This costs 50% of the credits you spent on the initial translation, and you can see a side by side comparative view.

To be completely honest... I generally don't bother. The AI translation model currently in use is very good. I do, on occasion, go back and proofread older translations which used an earlier version of the AI, when I have some spare credits, and reupload the book for sale. If you get some 'bad translation' reviews very early on, I'd definitely suggest going back and proofreading. Some languages may be better than others... if you notice that your average ratings are noticeably worse in Spanish, for example, it might be time to consider a round of proofing.

To Human Proofread, or Not?

You have a lot of options here. If you have a family member or friend who is a native speaker of your target language and is willing to have a read through for you? Definitely take them up on it. Otherwise, it's probably going to come down to budget. I found a couple of local fruit picking backpackers and gave them a bit of cash each to go over my first few translations!

You can find a human proofer in your target language on Fiverr, Upwork, or by word of mouth recommendation, or you can employ ProblemSolved (also known as Wordcount.ink) who are a professional translation company who work closely with ScribeShadow. I have friends who have used all of these methods and swear by them.

And... just as I said back in chapter two. Just like traditionally published books which have definitely been fully human translated by a professional translator, there will always be someone who leaves a critical review.

You can't please everyone.

And if you're a published author, you probably already know that. This is not to say that you shouldn't make the effort to try to put out a quality product, but... if you had a well-written and well-edited book to start with, a straight AI translation without further proofing is already going to be a pretty decent product. You can choose, depending on your budget and timelines, what you want to do. And remember; none of this is set in stone. It's pretty easy to upload an updated version on Amazon if you decide to do some more work on the translation later!

Reformatting

Some people take the epub straight from ScribeShadow and upload to Amazon, and I am mildly horrified by that idea because I like my books to look pretty internally. So I always import the translated .docx file back into Atticus (as a new book) and reformat with my chosen theme. This is where I add back in my translated copyright page and About The Author pages too.

Take a close look at your formatting. Drop caps look dreadful in some languages which use an em-dash to indicate a dialogue opening (like French), so if you have any chapter that opens with dialogue, you will definitely want to avoid drop caps.

I highly recommend you scroll through every chapter to check nothing has messed up... it's happened to me that the translation failed near the end of the chapter and the last few paragraphs didn't translate. Or some scene breaks got 'eaten' and the text 'image-placeholder' was left behind instead. And while this hasn't happened to me or any author I know doing AI translations, it's a recurring nightmare of mine that the AI might leave a prompt in the text... I have no desire to the be next viral joke on TikTok, thanks very much. Don't leave this to a human proofreader. You should always be the last line of defence for your book.

Back Matter

If you're an indie author, you already understand the importance of back matter in your book. Don't neglect it in translation! Start a newsletter list (yes, for each language) and put the signup link right after the end of the last chapter. It really doesn't take all that much time to run your newsletter through Chat to translate it and send it out to each sub-list every time you're sending it out. It's slow growing but those organic sign ups tend to be pretty loyal.

I like to direct my readers to the next book I want them to read – whether that's the next book in the series, book 1 in an entirely different series, or even a standalone book – by giving them not just the title, blurb and link, but also a free sample chapter, or partial chapter, and I make sure that sample ends on a nice hook. After this I have a simple phrase which translates as "Want to find out what happens next? Read [book title] now!"

Keep your back matter up to date. Reupload all books in your target language every time you have a new link to include in your "More Books by the Author" page, and make sure those links are universal links – you can get free ones by signing up to Books2Read. In Spanish especially, there are a lot of different Amazon stores your buyer might be wanting to purchase in. Don't force them to the .es (or worse, .com) store when they may not be shopping there.

Legal Obligations in the EU

... That's a really scary chapter heading, isn't it?

Disclaimer: I am not a lawyer, I don't even play one on TV, and the following should not be considered to constitute legal advice in ANY jurisdiction.

But there are things which you need to know if you're publishing books in the EU, and that means if you are selecting any EU Amazon store as your primary marketplace (which you will, in the next chapter). And this is something which you need to address at the formatting stage, because you are LEGALLY REQUIRED to provide the following:

A contact email address A contact postal address

And if you're selling a physical book, there must also be a contact name and postal address or a representative WITHIN THE EU.

That gave me conniptions at first, but fortunately, Amazon, Ingram and the various other POD (Print On Demand) printers do seem to have got somewhat organized about this. They have assured authors that they are 'handling this' by including, in books printed in the EU, those required details for a representative – I understand they are printed on the inside of the back cover.

(Again. Not a lawyer. And I haven't been able to source any official document from Amazon or any other printer which says this, so... maybe don't publish an AI-generated book about mushrooms which includes the kind of information which could get you sued. You don't want to be the FAFO person, do you?)

Some countries have different legal requirements. Germany, Austria and Switzerland are particularly hot on this; France, Italy, Spain and others not so much. But if you follow the advice I'm giving her, you SHOULD be covered.

(Once more. Not a lawyer!)

What YOU need to include in your translated book

A copyright statement, which includes what is sometimes also called an Impressum. If you look at the copyright page of this very book, you'll find one that I believe to satisfy the legal requirements for an author to publish ebooks and physical books within the EU, as long as your printer is also compliant as described above **(CHECK with your printer if you're doing special editions or a print run somewhere)**.

I've reproduced the copyright page here, and you're welcome to use it as a template... but obviously, substitute your own details for mine!

> Copyright © 2025 Shenanigans Press. All Rights Reserved.
> This book and all its contents are protected by copyright law. No part of this publication may be reproduced, distributed, or transmitted in any form or by any means, including photocopying, recording, or other electronic or mechanical methods, without the prior written permission of the publisher, except in the case of brief quotations used in reviews or other non-commercial uses permitted by copyright law.
> For permission requests, please contact:
> Shenanigans Press
> PO Box 323, MORAYFIELD QLD 4506 AUSTRALIA
> Email: cait@caitlynlynch.com

Of course, it's a good idea to translate your copyright page into your target language. But you only need to do this ONCE, which is why I delete the copyright pages when I upload the book to ScribeShadow – otherwise I'm just wasting credits unnecessarily. It's very simple to put your original copyright statement into ChatGPT, or even Google Translate is sufficient for this, and ask it to reproduce the statement in German or any other language.

New Requirement: Alt-Text for Informative Graphics in EU Ebooks (Effective June 28, 2025)

As of June 28, 2025, all ebooks published in the European Union must include **alt-text (alternative text descriptions) for any informative graphics**. This requirement is designed to improve accessibility for visually impaired readers, and it applies to all "informative" images in your ebook.

What does this mean for authors?

- If you write **non-fiction**, this will likely affect you the most, especially if you include charts, diagrams, or illustrations that convey important information.

- **Fiction authors** should also take note: if your book contains maps, family trees, timelines, or even text messages or emails presented as images, you must provide alt-text that conveys the essential information.

- Decorative images that do not convey information (such as flourishes or purely decorative illustrations) do not require alt-text; they are not considered 'informative'.

What is alt-text?

Alt-text is a short, written description of an image that is

embedded in the ebook's file. Screen readers use alt-text to describe images to visually impaired users. For example, for a map in a fantasy novel, your alt-text might say:
"A hand-drawn black and white map showing the island kingdom of Eldoria, with major cities marked: Rivertown in the north, Goldharbour in the west, and Dragonspire in the south."

How do I add alt-text?

Some modern ebook formatting tools (Atticus and Vellum definitely, not sure about others) allow you to add alt-text when you insert an image. If you use a formatter, make sure they are aware of this requirement for EU publications.

Failure to comply may result in your ebook being delisted from EU retailers or being inaccessible to some readers.

Amazon now have a section when you upload that you must check off (see screenshot below).

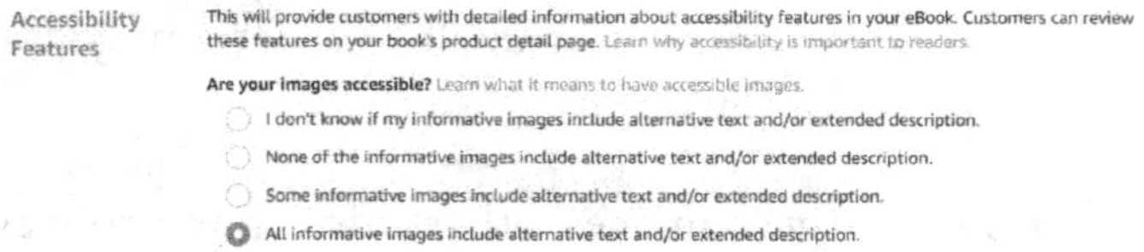

You must check the last box if you are publishing a new book to the EU. You should update older books when possible, especially if you are reuploading to update backmatter.

It's OK to still check this box IF you have purely decorative images and they don't have alt-text, because they are not considered 'informative'.

Latest information is that Google Play have added something similar. It will be on all ebook uploading platforms before long, if it isn't already.

I have existing translations; do I need to update all those to comply with this new rule?

Current EU guidance states that ebooks 'placed on the market' (i.e., first published/made available for sale) before June 28, 2025, are not required to be retroactively updated.

However, **if you make substantial updates or re-release an existing ebook after June 28, 2025** – for example, uploading a new edition, changing the cover, or altering the content – **that version is considered a 'new product' and must comply with the accessibility requirements, including alt-text**.

I don't know how picky they're going to be about this, but I am personally going to err on the side of caution. Even if I'm just updating backmatter links, that is 'altering the content'. I'll be ensuring that I don't have any 'informative images' in the book, adding alt-text if I do, and checking that bottom box on Amazon.

This regulation actually applies even to your English-language books with Amazon US selected as the primary market.
If EU readers can buy your book, the law applies.

I've heard about GDPR – what's that?

GDPR applies if you are **collecting personal information** from people in the European Union, such as when you gather email addresses for a newsletter sign-up list. There are a few more legal hoops to jump through if you're doing that, but the basics are:

- You need a **privacy statement** on your website.
- You must clearly explain **what people are signing up for**, at the time when they sign up.
- People must be able to **unsubscribe easily** at any time.
- You are legally required to keep their data secure and not share it or use it for any purpose other than what they agreed to when they signed up.

These are best practices you should be following anyway. I'm not going into further detail here, as the topic is outside the scope of this book. But if you plan to invite readers to join your email list, make sure you're compliant with GDPR and other relevant privacy regulations.

For more information, organizations like the Information Commissioner's Office (ICO) provide free guidance for small businesses and individuals.

READY, SET, SELL

Preparing Your Covers

As I noted earlier, there is a school of thought that says you don't actually have to translate the English title and you can use the same cover for every language. I personally think this feels like something of a cop-out. If you cannot change your covers (because you can't afford to or your cover artist won't play ball) then you might have to. Or maybe you've got a series where each book title is literally just a character name... fine, in that case. Just make sure that you can use that title in German. Remember, it has to be a unique title, so you might need to incorporate the series name as a subtitle.

I like to translate the titles because each translated book is a unique product and it helps me to differentiate them. If I had 6 books all with the same title I think I'd lose my mind in confusion. But I am my own cover artist for 90% of my books, and for the others I have a cover artist who makes a nominal charge to swap out the cover text for each language, as long as I send her all the languages at once so she can do it all in one session.

Talk to your cover artist and negotiate, if you can't do this for yourself. Whatever you do, don't do anything silly like remove the text in Canva and put new text on yourself... you probably don't have the rights to do this and your cover artist will be righteously annoyed that you've infringed on their copyright!

Paperbacks in French and Spanish – A Local Quirk

Did you know that in French and Spanish, the spine text on the cover is the other way up? Look at a paperback in English and the spine text reads from 'top to bottom', usually with the title at the top of the spine and the author name at the bottom. If you lay the book down with the cover facing up and look at the spine, the text is the right way up to read.

But in French and Spanish, the spine is oriented the other way around. The title is usually still at the 'top' and the author name at the bottom, but the text is inverted so that you read from 'bottom to top'. I've put in a graphic below to illustrate how this works. Doing this might seem like a small thing, but to French and Spanish readers, it will make you seem more legitimate. Your books will look 'right' on their shelves among the traditionally published ones, and they'll be more likely to come back and buy from you again... and remember, paperback sales may be a significantly higher percentage of your total for these translations than you might normally find in the English-speaking markets.

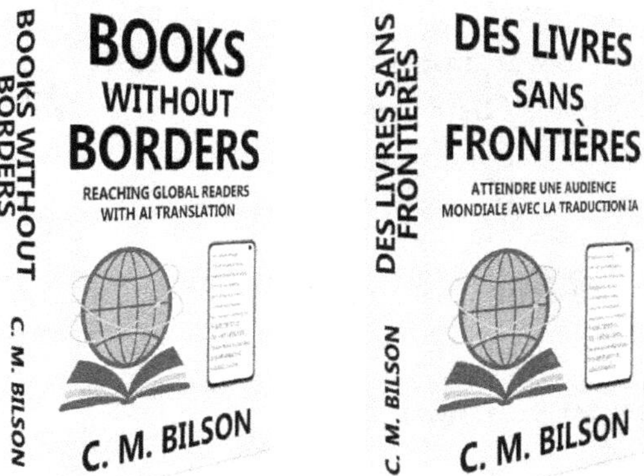

Uploading to Sales Platforms

I'm assuming that if you're looking to monetise your backlist with translations, you already know how to go about uploading your book to the various sales platforms, and that you're making your own informed decisions about whether to enrol your book in Kindle Unlimited or to sell wide.

> Each translation is considered to be an entirely separate product, so the exclusivity clause for Kindle Unlimited doesn't apply to different translations of the same book.

So it's completely possible to have English and French versions of your book in Kindle Unlimited, and be wide with German, Italian and Spanish. And you should definitely put paperbacks wide; I upload mine through both KDP Print (don't check the Expanded Distribution box) and Draft2Digital Print. Both provide free ISBNs. You will, however, need your own ISBN to upload to Ingram Spark and possibly for other sites (see the chapter on Paperback Distribution for why you probably want to).

Note that the Amazon.nl store doesn't have Kindle Unlimited: definitely don't enrol any Dutch books in KU!

Where to sell wide?

Every country has their own ebook store which their citizens seem to prefer, if they aren't shopping at Amazon. But you can get lost in having accounts at 20 different stores, some of which will never repay the time and effort spent uploading there. So here are my suggestions:

Amazon KDP (don't enroll in KDP Select if you're going wide!)
Google Play
Kobo Writing Life (enroll in Kobo Plus)
Tolino (for German editions)
Apple Books – maybe. I haven't cracked the Apple code, so I just use D2D to distribute to Apple.
AuthorFreely – for Brazilian editions, and ONLY if you are in Australia or New Zealand, to get into Brazilian bookstores. See the Paperback Distribution chapter for more information on this topic.
Draft2Digital for everywhere else, unchecking the stores

you are going direct to

Setting the Language

I bet you haven't even noticed, but when you click Create a New Kindle book on Amazon KDP, the first question you have to fill in isn't the book title. It's what language the book is written in. And other distribution platforms also have this question on the first page. Make sure you pick the correct language.

kindle direct publishing
Bookshelf
Reports
Community
Marketing
Kindle eBook Details
In Progress...
Kindle eBook Content
Not Started...
Kindle eBook Pricing
Not Started...
Language
Choose the primary language your book is written in. Supported languages
English
Book Title
Enter your title as it appears on the book cover. If you add a subtitle, a colon will be inserted between the title and subtitle. Before continuing, check your spelling since this field cannot be updated after publication. Book title guidelines
Book Title

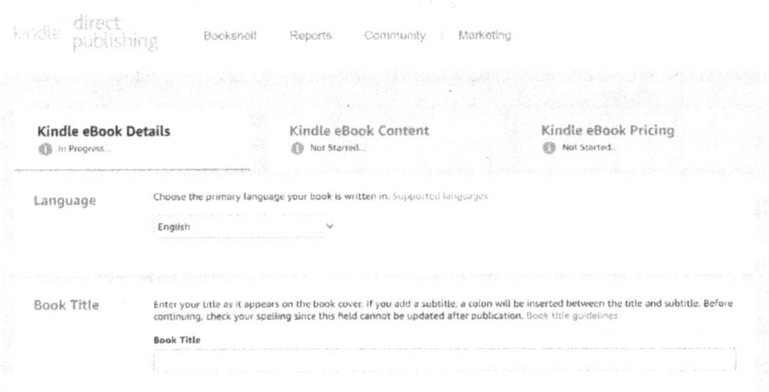

Further down the page, under the blurb, you need to select the Primary Marketplace for your book.

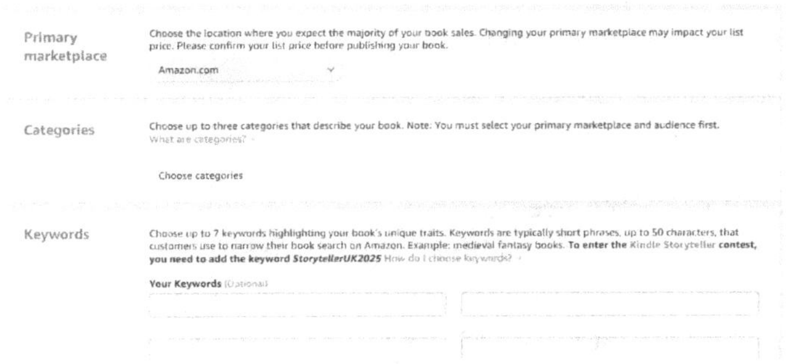

Primary marketplace
Choose the location where you expect the majority of your book sales. Changing your primary marketplace may impact your list price. Please confirm your list price before publishing your book.
Amazon.com
Categories
Choose up to three categories that describe your book. Note: You must select your primary marketplace and audience first.
What are categories?
Choose categories
Keywords
Choose up to 7 keywords highlighting your book's unique traits. Keywords are typically short phrases, up to 50 characters, that customers use to narrow their book search on Amazon. Example: medieval fantasy books. To enter the Kindle Storyteller contest, you need to add the keyword StorytellerUK2025 How do I choose keywords?
Your Keywords (Optional)

For German, you will select amazon.de
French, amazon.fr
Spanish, amazon.es
Italian, amazon.it
Brazil, amazon.com.br
Dutch, amazon.nl
Etc. etc.

It is important to make this selection before you choose your categories, because *categories are different in the various Amazon stores.*

This can be one of the most painful parts of the process – I'm sure you know the best categories for your book in your home store, but they might not even exist in your target country.

A particularly annoying one is Regency Romance in France: the Romance - Historical subcategories in French do not include Regency as an available timeframe for ebooks, but it does exist in paperbacks. No, I don't know why. And ebook and paperbook categories may be differently named in the same country store – for example, if you write Clean Romance, in Germany you'd probably use the "Liebesromane › Liebesroman (Wholesome Romance)" category in ebook, but "Liebesromane › Leichte Kost" in paperback.

You'll probably need to spend a bit of time puzzling this out. I copy-paste available categories into Google Translate regularly when trying to work out what categories to select in different countries. Once you have them, make a note of them! Assuming you mostly write in the same genre, you won't want to go through this process every time you upload another book in German.

This is also where you're going to put in the keywords in your target language which you worked out in that conversation with ChatGPT where you figured out your titles and blurbs.

On the next page, once you've uploaded your files, comes the question about AI content. If you've never had to check Yes here before, you should now. Be honest. Amazon doesn't share this information with customers at the present time; it's for internal use only, but it is part of the terms and conditions that you need to tell them. I fill in as below:

If you've had the translation human proofed or edited, you can select "Entire work, with extensive editing" instead.

Set your pricing on the next page and push that Publish button!

It's not too different on Draft2Digital, Kobo, and Google Play. Things might be in a slightly different order, but you'll still need to fill in metadata, select language, put in blurb, categories and keywords, choose language, upload your files, and enter pricing.

Paperback Distribution and Special Editions

I talked a little about this in the previous chapter but it's worth delving into a little more deeply, because as indie authors, I think we often leave a lot of money on the table when it comes to physical editions.

But here's a few cold, hard statistics.

Print books make up **~75% to 80%** of total global book market revenue.

Ebooks account for **~15% to 20%** of global book market revenue.

Audiobooks are growing, making up **~5–8%** in major English-speaking markets, but are still a small part globally.

Print books remain the overwhelming preference worldwide, especially outside the U.S. and U.K., and for genres like children's books and nonfiction.

Ebook growth has plateaued in many mature markets, but print continues to see strong demand.

Those are GLOBAL statistics.

Let's have a look at some of the specific countries we're talking about marketing to with our translations.

COUNTRY	PRINT BOOKS: AMAZON MARKET SHARE	EBOOKS: AMAZON MARKET SHARE	EBOOKS AS % OF TOTAL MARKET	NOTES
Germany	20-25%	60-70%	~6%	
France	15-18%	~60%	~7%	
Italy	15-20%	60-70%	<10%	
Spain	10-15%	~70%	5-6%	
Netherlands	~5%	10-15%	5-7%	Amazon.nl does not have KU; Amazon small in ebooks
Brazil	(N/A; Amazon does not print)	70-80%	5-8%	Amazon does not print in Brazil; dominates ebooks

Conclusion:
Ebooks are between 5 and 10% of the TOTAL book market share by revenue in these countries.

But... how do I get into bookstores to get some of that 90+% market share?

That's the age-old indie author problem, of course, and it's complicated by the fact that you're probably in a whole different country and don't speak the language. You can't wander into your local bookstore and ask to speak to the manager.

But remember this. Many of these countries quite simply don't have the choices of books that are available in English. If you're running ads to your books, you absolutely should be including links to where buyers can buy your physical books online. And if that's only on Amazon, that's okay – looking at the above figures, Amazon do have about 50% of that online book sales market in most EU markets. Listing through Ingram Spark and/or Draft2Digital, however, will get you listed on the other major big bookstores' online catalogues. Here's a non-comprehensive list of the most popular big bookstores in these markets:

Germany: Thalia, Buecher.de, Weltbild, Hugendubel, Osiander

France: FNAC, Cultura, Decitre, Furet du Nord

Italy: IBS, LaFeltrinelli, Mondadori, Hoepli

Spain: Casa del Libro, FNAC, El Corte Inglés, Agapea

The Netherlands: Bol, Bruna, Libris, Paagman, Boekhandel De Slegte

But not Brazil?

Not Brazil. That's another problem to solve, and one which I'm still figuring out. Ingram do apparently have POD in Brazil, but limited reach as yet, and the biggest physical bookstores in the country – Submarino, Americanas, and Cultura – are challenging for indies as these typically only stock books from major publishers and large distributors.

The biggest POD printer in the country (the local version of Ingram, it seems) is Club de Autores, who are also a major online bookseller... and **I'm about to let you into a little secret**, which, *if you're in Australia or New Zealand*, might just be very helpful.

(Sorry, to the Americans, Canadians, Brits etc. out there. Look, you get lots of things. Us Aussies can't even sign up for ACX to make audiobooks. You gotta let us have this one.)

If you go to Club de Autores website and try to sign up for an account to publish books, sadly you'll discover that you have to have a Brazilian bank account to get paid, and that's quite tricky for non-Brazilians (and may have tax implications you don't want to deal with). But up along the top of that website there's a banner with a list of different countries... Brazil, Portugal, Australia/New Zealand, Spain and Germany. And if you click on the Australia/New Zealand one, you'll find yourself on an English-language version of the Club de Autores website called Author Freely, who just launched in March 2025. It's not difficult at all to sign up for an account and publish your paperback there (though you'll probably have to reformat your interior and resize your cover as they only have slightly painful sizes), but that will get your book available to print and sell from Club de Autores.

I've been talking to Author Freely, and this is the information they shared with me.

> "By uploading your book to Author Freely, your book will automatically be made available for sale on the Club de Autores bookstore and affiliated retailers including but not limited to Mercado Livre, Americanas.com, Shoptime, Estante Virtual, and the usual Amazon, Apple, Google Play and Kobo."

They don't appear to offer any promotional opportunities at this time... but I asked the question, which might start them thinking about it!

Special Editions

I should probably have a T-shirt saying 'I Love Pretty Books'.

Look, we all know that the special edition market has taken off, ever since Fourth Wing launched and EVERYONE wanted a pretty book with dragons on the edges. Especially in fantasy romance, many indie authors are producing their own beautiful editions, often running Kickstarters to fund their print runs and then selling from their own online shops and at book conventions.

But once again, foreign markets are underserved in this area.

Even the traditionally published book market isn't doing many sprayed-edge books in translation, and readers are

HUNGRY for them. Go look at #BooktokBrasil for a while and it won't take you long to realise that the moment somebody holds up a pretty special edition, the comments are full of "WHERE DID YOU GET IT???" and "OMG I NEED ONE!!!" (in Portuguese, of course).

And it's the same in the other international markets.

But special editions... that's hard. Big print runs, Chinese printers, storage, shipping...

Yes. And also no.

Below are a few options that are less painful, and a lot less upfront expense than a 300+ book print run.

Bookvault (UK based) can do POD special editions with all the bells and whistles of foiling and sprayed edges, and ship them to the EU. Yes, the books won't be cheap. But if you can generate the demand... and remember, you won't actually PAY for the books unless you sell them, with POD. There's not a whole lot of upfront outlay.

Booksfactory are based in Poland. They'll do print runs of fancy special editions pretty darn cheaply (by comparison to Bookvault), for runs as short as 20 books. Yes, you then run into a distribution issue, but if you've run a Kickstarter and have the orders, it shouldn't be all that tricky to get on Upwork and hire someone locally to handle the fulfilment end of things for you.

Note; while Kickstarter, Indiegogo and Patreon are technically global platforms, they are not the most

popular crowdfunding platforms in non-English speaking countries. Here's some you should look at for our target nations:

Germany: Startnext, VisionBakery

France: Ulele, KissKissBankBank

Italy: Produzioni dal Basso, Eppela

Spain: Verkami, Goteo

Portugal: PPL

The Netherlands: Voordekunst

Brazil: Catarse, Benfeitoria

Consider using a distribution agent

A what now? Well, this is pretty much a brand new job description, but a fellow author who's based in Germany has decided to see if she can make it work. She's already got contacts with some of the big bookshop buyers in Germany and Spain, and is working on France and Italy, and let me tell you these buyers are VERY interested in getting their hands on special editions for their customers to snatch up and coo over on Instagram and TikTok. Anastasia is still setting up exactly how this is going to work, but the current plan is to print at Booksfactory and deliver directly to the big bookstores' distribution hubs, and they'll take it from there.

Visit cowperauthorservices.com/author-services for

up-to-date information.

Forced edge POD editions

If you have Vellum, you probably know about the new update that enables you to insert forced edges, but it's still pretty complicated to do. If you use a service like PrintedEdges.com, however, you don't even need Vellum. It costs $20 per book (and you can use the same file for paperback and hardback, FYI) and they'll walk you through it all, and then you can just upload the PDF to Ingram and voilà, you have a special edition POD.

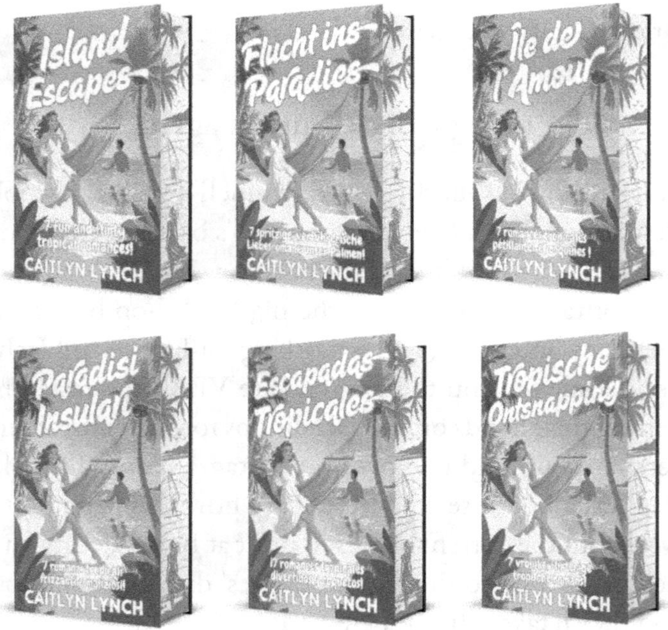

I might be biased, but I think they look pretty darn nice...

and they are no more expensive than a standard paperback or hardback POD book. This one is a greyscale design because colour printing every page DOES mount up, but it's definitely possible.

While it's *theoretically* possible to get KDP Print to do these as well, I'm finding it utterly painful. Occasionally they'll let one through, but usually they reject the interior file and will not listen to explanations, insisting that you remove 'color registration marks' which are nothing of the sort. I've basically given up and just upload them to Ingram now, and then contact Author Central to get editions linked together for the product sales page.

A+ content really comes into its own here. You can only put A+ content on books published through KDP, so just do it on your ebook, but you can do a side-by-side comparison of the editions available, which means that anyone ending up on your ebook page in the Kindle store is going to be SHOWN that there are pretty editions available. Don't neglect it. It's worth the effort.

¡Encuentra tu edición perfecta!

Lee al instante – Edición ebook

Disfruta la serie completa de Las Novias Ruborizadas en cualquier momento y lugar desde tu dispositivo favorito. Acceso inmediato a las cuatro dulces novelas románticas en una cómoda edición digital.

Edición especial en rústica

Libro en rústica que reúne los cuatro títulos de la serie Las Novias Ruborizadas. Incluye cantos impresos y 530 páginas de historias románticas, adecuado para cualquier momento de lectura.

Tapa dura de lujo para coleccionistas

Edición en tapa dura que recopila la serie completa Las Novias Ruborizadas en un solo volumen. Incluye cantos impresos y diseño cuidado, con 530 páginas de historias románticas.

I must emphasize that a lot of the advice in this chapter is theoretical at this point of time. Indie

authors are, as usual, having to trailblaze how this is going to work, and we're still puzzling it out – but the tools exist, and the market is definitely there. Don't put it in the 'too hard' basket and forget about it.

> ***Readers out there want your books in their languages, and they want them physically in their hands and on their shelves, and they want them in pretty special editions.***
> ***"If you build it, they will come."***

Sources for the data provided in this chapter:

Statista, Global Book Market Revenue Share 2023

WordsRated, Ebook Market Share & Sales Statistics 2024

Börsenverein des Deutschen Buchhandels - Buchmarkt Zahlen 2023

SNE, Marché du livre 2023

Associazione Italiana Editori - Rapporto sullo Stato dell'Editoria 2023

FGEE, Informe 2023

PublishNews, 2023

CB Annual Report 2023

Boekblad: "Amazon krijgt geen voet aan de grond in Nederlandse boekenmarkt" (2023)

Real Results, Real Money

I was genuinely surprised when I released my first translations in French and German and sales and KU page reads began to trickle in with no promotion whatsoever.

But the real results came when I put out a full series and started ads.

This is a screenshot from my KDP dashboard. Can you guess what happened at points 1, 2, and 3?

Point 1 was the release of my first translations.
Point 2 was the release of the 4-book series in German; I

started Facebook ads a day later with a $10/day budget. Point 3 was the release of the series in French; Facebook ads started a day later with a $10/day budget.

Total ad spend across the period shown was about $1,000.

Have I got your attention now?

(And no, I didn't have 291 books out. I had 48, many of them short novellas. 291 is the current total counting most of those books now translated, plus several I've written since).

> In July 2024, I made $2,367.45
> In August 2024, I made $12,857.73
> In September 2024, I made $22,112.68
>
> and this life-changing increase in income was entirely due to translations.

My costs: I'd spent about $500 on ScribeShadow subscriptions, about $500 cash-in-hand to my backpacker proofreaders, and about $1,000 in ad spend. So: $2,000 to increase my income by almost $20,000. For me, that was literally life-changing – I was able to upgrade my 13-year-old car and bank a couple of months' mortgage payments. It meant I could take a breath, for the first time in a long time, and start thinking long term instead of worrying day-to-day about finances.

I'm not trying to sell you on some pyramid scheme here. I don't have a fancy course to upsell you to, and I don't make any money directly from ScribeShadow – the only way I profit there is if you choose to use my affiliate link to sign up. I'm just here to show you what's possible using a fairly inexpensive tool and your existing backlist.

I'm also not making any guarantees. As I noted earlier, translations won't transform a donkey into a racehorse (to steal a metaphor from Indie megaseller Elana Johnson). You still need a good book (ideally a series) which is written to market, with a marketable cover and a well-written blurb, and if you want big results you will probably need to be running ads; whether you run Facebook ads or Amazon ads will depend on your skillset and your budget (and whether you are wide or in KU). *

* unless you're one of those social media mavens who can kill it on TikTok and Instagram in multiple languages. You go, legend!

I've never run ads and I don't know where to start: help me!

David Gaughran has a fantastic free video series on Youtube about Facebook ads.

Dave Chesson at Kindlepreneur has a free Amazon ads course.

If you've never tried either before, those would be my go-to references to get started, because you really can't beat free, right? I'm not providing links because links break (and are useless in paperbacks anyway) but Google is also free.

I have no budget!

Do you have $30? You can start with Facebook ads from $1 a day, so $30 would be your budget for the first month. Try a small ad in French or German. Once you've recouped your investment and hopefully at least doubled what you put in, you can creep your ad spend up. Or start an ad in another language.

I didn't start off spending $150 a day, but that's where I'm at now, and I know people who started at $5 a day and are now spending 4 figures (to make 5 figures... yes, every day!).

And if you REALLY have no money, but you have time... get onto Instagram and TikTok and see if you can't crack that algorithm.

Marketplace Pricing and KU Page Rates: What You Need to Know

When preparing your translated books for global release, it's important to remember that ebook pricing is not universal. Every Amazon marketplace has its own recommended price ranges and local economic realities. A price that works in the US or UK may absolutely not for readers in France, Brazil, or India.

One especially important factor is **Kindle Unlimited (KU) page-read rates**, which vary from country to country. Each month, Amazon sets a different KENP (Kindle Edition Normalized Page) rate for every KU region. Some countries, like Germany and France, pay rates that are close to those in the US and UK. Others, such as Brazil, Mexico, or India, may pay out only a fraction of what you would earn per page read in higher-paying markets. In Brazil, for example, the KENP rate is regularly as little as 30% of the US rate.

I'm not including specific comparison rates here because they change monthly, but if you go to https://readerlinks.com/kenp_rates/index.phpyou should be able to see the most recent month's calculations.

This means that even if you see strong page-read numbers in certain countries, your actual royalties might not be as high as you expect. It is not uncommon for authors to be surprised by lower earnings from high-volume KU countries with lower payout rates.

What does this mean for your translation strategy?

- Keep an eye on the *current* KENP rates for each country where your book is enrolled in KU. These rates are published each month and they do fluctuate.

- Consider whether KU is the best option for every market. In some countries, you may earn more by going wide instead of enrolling in KU.

- Take time to adjust your ebook and paperback prices for each marketplace, considering local taxes (like VAT or GST), currency conversion, and Amazon's minimum and maximum price requirements.

- Remember that some markets, such as the Netherlands, do not offer KU at all. In those markets, your only option is to publish wide.

- Track your sales and KU reads by country to understand where your income is coming from and to make informed decisions about your pricing and distribution.

> When uploading your book, use Amazon's regional pricing tools to review and set prices for each marketplace individually, rather than relying on automatic conversions from your home currency. This small step can make your books more competitive and attractive to international readers.
>
> Staying aware of these differences and regularly checking KDP's latest KU rate announcements will help you maximize your income and avoid surprises as you expand your books' reach around the world.

CASE STUDIES

When I decided to write this book, I put out a call in the ScribeShadow Facebook group (highly recommend you join, so much knowledge and so many people who are very kind with even the most dim-witted questions) asking if any authors would be willing to share some of their results and experiences, so this book wasn't just me making claims based off only my own experiences.

I promised anonymity (...because trolls) and therefore, you won't find any author names or book titles. I assigned each contributing author a random letter and will refer to them simply as "Author A" or similar, though I have included the genres they write in, because specific genres do perform better in some markets than others.

While I was not able to use all of the case studies I received as this book needs to be a sensible length, I tried to select a good variation, from authors with only a few books to those with dozens, people translating in one language only to others experimenting beyond the

ScribeShadow languages, and authors writing in different genres (though almost all the respondents were writing in romance subgenres). I also included people who aren't, in my opinion, doing very well, to demonstrate that this is not a one-size-fits-all technique to suddenly become successful beyond your wildest dreams. That's the kind of scam vanity publishers try to sell you on, and as I mentioned way back at the beginning of this book, I have good reason not to be very fond of vanity publishers and their ilk.

While I formatted and lightly edited responses for consistency and clarity, I did not remove or alter any of the authors' responses (unless to preserve anonymity) even when their suggestions and experiences are radically different to my own.

I hope the following information may be useful for you to make your own decisions about how to proceed on your translation journey.

I have occasionally added clarifying comments in italics.

I have added a small analysis at the end of each case study in bold italics.

Case Study: Author E

Genre: Regency Romance

Number of Books Published in English: 14 (all novellas)

Languages Translated Into: French, Italian, German, Spanish

Number of Books Translated (per language):

12 in all 4 languages
6 in French and Italian

Series or Standalones: Technically standalones, but grouped into 2 x 6-book series by theme

Distribution Approach: Kindle Unlimited

Promotion:

- No ads for most languages so far

- Just started Facebook ads for Spanish (May 2025); CPC only €0.04 but haven't seen much impact yet

Proofreading/Quality Assurance:

None used; raw output from ScribeShadow, reformatted in Vellum.

Average Monthly Sales/Profit:

- French translations performed exceptionally well with no advertising

Author E kindly provided an evidentiary screenshot, for 10 of their books in French. $940.94 Australian, in 6 months, without ad support.

Surprises/Challenges:

- French books went bonkers with no advertising!

- French sales have slowed down, now considering advertising for the first time
- Spain/Spanish translations have underperformed, even with ads
- Advertising now started in Spanish because it was the worst performing language

Workflow Tips & Advice:

- Pick one language and do several books in one hit; that way your new readers will see you have a few books to read. I feel this is better than doing one book in multiple languages.

Quote:

"This is an absolute game changer for me. Things have started to die down, so I am only now starting with advertising."

My analysis: A solid small-scale, low-budget approach. Novellas can be a hard sell but 'chaining' them as themed series can work quite well. Small-scale ads should help Author E grow their profits.

Case Study: Author P

Genre: Mysteries – cozy and detective series (plus romantic women's fiction, not yet translated)

Number of Books Published in English: 37

Languages Translated Into: German, Italian, French, Spanish

Number of Books Translated (per language):

German: 4 (1 series)
French: 9 (2 series)
Italian: 9 (2 series)
Spanish: 4 (1 series)

Series or Standalones: Series (one with four titles, one with five titles)

Distribution Approach: Kindle Unlimited

Advertising:

- Both Facebook Ads and Amazon Ads
- Ads run in German, Italian, French, Spanish
- All ads are effective, but German's effectiveness is waning

Proofreading/Quality Assurance:

Human proofreader/editor (ProblemSolved)

Average Monthly Sales/Profit:

- German: approx $1,000 USD per month (55% page reads)
- Italian: approx $1,200 USD per month (65% page reads)
- French: approx $2,000 USD per month (65% page reads)
- Spanish: $500 USD per month (75% page reads, only one month of data)

Author P kindly provided the screenshot below, which shows some spectacular results. Over $21,000 US in 5 months!

Of course, these results don't come free. Author P also provided a Facebook ad spend screenshot for the same period.

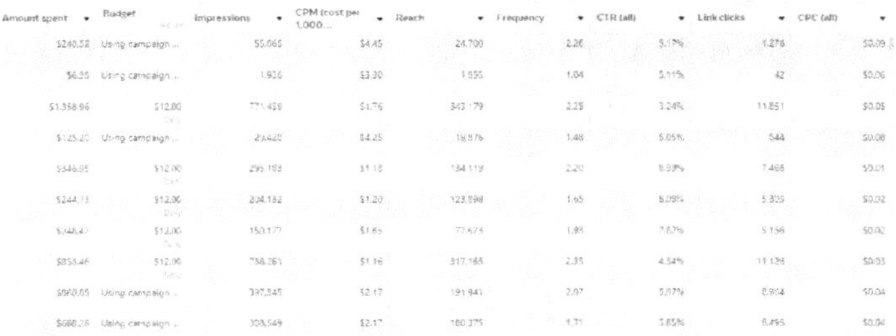

Amount spent	Budget	Impressions	CPM (cost per 1,000...	Reach	Frequency	CTR (all)	Link clicks	CPC (all)
$240.58	Using campaign ...	55,065	$4.45	24,700	2.26	5.17%	1,276	$0.09
$6.35	Using campaign ...	1,936	$3.30	1,855	1.04	5.11%	42	$0.06
$1,358.96	$12.00 Daily	771,439	$1.76	343,179	2.25	3.24%	11,851	$0.05
$125.20	Using campaign ...	29,420	$4.25	19,876	1.48	5.05%	544	$0.08
$346.95	$12.00	295,183	$1.18	134,119	2.20	8.93%	7,468	$0.01
$244.73	$12.00 Daily	204,182	$1.20	123,898	1.65	6.09%	5,335	$0.02
$248.47	$12.00	150,177	$1.65	77,673	1.93	7.67%	5,156	$0.02
$855.46	$12.00	738,261	$1.16	317,165	2.33	4.34%	11,128	$0.03
$860.65	Using campaign ...	397,345	$2.17	191,941	2.07	5.07%	8,904	$0.04
$668.26	Using campaign ...	308,549	$2.17	180,375	1.71	3.65%	8,495	$0.04

Look at the cost-per-clicks in the right-hand column! Anyone used to using Facebook ads in the US probably just fainted.

Surprises/Challenges:

- Germany was the first market and did incredibly well for six months, then it became harder to keep traction. Facebook ads not as responsive as before, so now also trying Amazon ads
- France and Italy continue to grow with only one

Facebook ad for each first-in-series and occasional Amazon ads

- Lower ratings than English books are common, but sales and reads remain strong

- Spanish is new but shows growth; Facebook ads are surprisingly low cost

- Trolls leave 1-star reviews on anything they suspect is machine-translated; some even quote inaccurate passages in reviews. Amazon has removed these when reported

Workflow Tips & Advice:

- If using human proofreaders, allow them enough time or stockpile series for rapid release

- Double-check language and market settings (e.g., German/Germany for German) and target-market pricing

- Advertising in other countries with the same official language (e.g., Canada for French) can be worth it, just narrow by language

- Ensure covers fit the target market, and that front/back matter is well translated and leads to other books

- Start ads targeting your ideal demographic immediately

Quote:

"As with my English titles I aim for the best reader experience I can provide. I find it is worth the extra time to ensure my covers fit the target market, that front and backmatter is well translated and leads readers to my other books, and that I immediately start ads targeting the readers who tend to fit my demographic."

My analysis: This author is absolutely killing it. Well set up for long-term success.

Case Study: Author M

(A French native speaker translating from English to French)

Genre: Sweet romcom

Number of Books Published in English: 16

Languages Translated Into: French

Number of Books Translated (per language): 8 (publishing one per month)

Series or Standalones: Interconnected standalones

Distribution Approach: Kindle Unlimited

Promotion:

Facebook Ads (5€/day), Instagram (just started)

Proofreading/Quality Assurance:

Human proofreader/editor (the author, native French speaker)

Average Monthly Sales/Profit:

427€ on the latest release (first month), 302€ net

Surprises/Challenges:

- More work than expected, even as a native speaker
- Fun and rewarding to reach new readers

Workflow Tips & Advice:

- Newsletters work well in France
- Always use a native proofreader for fiction, especially in French and German
- AI is great for a first draft but not publishable as-is for fiction

Quote:

"Definitely hire a human reviewer (native who understands fiction) for French and from what I've heard German too. I can only say for sure in France but, while the AI is a fantastic tool for a first draft, it's definitely not qualitative enough to be published as is, except maybe for non fiction. But the AI struggles with nuances, jokes, idioms, punctuations etc."

My analysis: A slow and cautious approach which is showing steady profitability. Nice work!

Case Study: Author C

Genre: Romance

Number of Books Published in English: 33

Languages Translated Into: French, German, Dutch, Spanish, Italian, Portuguese

Number of Books Translated (per language):
French 12
German 12
Portuguese 12

Series or Standalones: Series

Distribution Approach: Wide (Kobo, Apple, Google, etc.)

(Tried Kindle Unlimited for Portuguese but will not do it again.)

Promotion:

- No ads currently, but maintains country-specific social media accounts and strategies (e.g., TikTok, Instagram)
- Other ad methods
- Not running ads at the moment; previously ran $50/day Facebook ads for German translations (saw strong initial results, then tapering)

Proofreading/Quality Assurance:

- ScribeShadow AI proofreading
- Human proofreader/editor
- Bilingual beta reader
- Used husband for Portuguese; hired professional service (Problem Solved) for German

Average Monthly Sales/Profit:

Not running ads currently; about $50/month in German and $50/month in French

Surprises/Challenges:

- Initially did very well with German translations and high Facebook ad spend, but sales tapered off - possibly due to disclosure of AI translation
- Switched to paying for human rechecks
- Brazilian Portuguese was a total money sinkhole

and not worth it

Workflow Tips & Advice:

- Used ScribeShadow, but also ran chapters through ChatGPT in the target language to check readability
- Used ChatGPT to adapt puns and wordplay that didn't translate well
- Recommend quality control before publishing

Quote:

"I paid ScribeShadow, but then would put a chapter or two in ChatGPT and ask how it read in whatever language I wanted to ask about. I'd also separately use ChatGPT to rename things that didn't translate well – like puns and crossword puzzles."

My analysis: A fairly steady approach, but $50/day is a huge amount to be spending in one language and I'm not surprised results fell off quickly. Disclosure of AI translation isn't required and, as this author found, can badly adversely affect sales. My advice is DON'T. Brazil can be a tough market to crack; my experience is Brazilian readers do not buy books at all, they only read in KU.

Case Study: Author G

Author G has used DeepL as well as ScribeShadow to translate to MANY languages

Genre: Paranormal romance, romantasy, science fiction romance, steamy romcom, romantic suspense

Number of Books Published in English: 100+ books

Languages Translated Into: German, French, Italian, Dutch, Spanish, Brazilian Portuguese, Catalan, Swedish, Hungarian, Indonesian, Czech, Danish, Estonian, Finnish, Russian, Romanian, Polish, Turkish, Latvian, Lithuanian, Slovak, Slovenian, Norwegian, Chinese, Hindi, Thai, Japanese, Arabic

Number of Books Translated (per language): Approximately 40 in all the above languages, plus another 40 in German, French, Dutch, Italian, Spanish, Brazilian Portuguese, Russian, Chinese, Thai, Hindi, and Japanese

Series or Standalones: All are in series

Distribution Approach: Wide

Distributed through as many channels as possible, including PublishDrive, Draft2Digital, Amazon, Kobo, Findaway, and Google Play

Advertising:

- Facebook Ads in French, German, and Dutch; tried ads in Italian and Spanish, but saw profit only in French, German, and Dutch
- French and German ads for paranormal romance and science fiction romance
- Dutch ads for paranormal romance and steamy romcom

Proofreading/Quality Assurance:

None.

Average Monthly Sales/Profit:

- Net about $5,000 a month, average, in the 10 months since starting translations
- Monthly net varies from $3,000 to $8,000
- Facebook ad spend is $2,000–$3,000 per month

Surprises/Challenges:

- Dutch was a surprise success, especially on Kobo Plus
- Spanish AI-generated audiobooks performed well on Findaway Voices *(note; Findaway Voices only distribute to limited markets as not all stores accept AI-generated audio. You have to have a separate account now to distribute to Spotify as well.)*
- Czech, Hungarian, and Polish have done well with no ads for two science fiction romance series (*DeepL translations*)
- Planning to try PNR next in those languages and commence ads.

Workflow Tips & Advice:

- Testing new genres and languages can reveal unexpected markets
- Running ads in new languages can dramatically increase income (10x ROI in some cases)
- Consider trying multiple platforms and formats (including audiobooks)

Quote:

"Czech, Hungarian and Polish have done well for me so far, with no ads, for the two SFR series I've released. Going to try PNR next, then FB ads as that 10x my translation income when I did that for French and German."

My analysis: Holy moly! Talk about conquering the entire world! That's 28 languages by my count; that's some force multiplier! Author G did not specify, but I'm guessing they may be using a free-first-in-series strategy in many languages to help get eyes on their books. I don't even want to THINK about how complicated their titles-and-links spreadsheets must be, with that many languages!

While initially this might appear to be a pretty wild, throwing spaghetti-at-the-wall approach, note that Author G is analysing what works and what hasn't, and is narrowing down their approach to focus on specific genres and markets. With a large and diversified backlist, they have an excellent chance of 'cornering the market' in some of those languages. I'm fascinated to see how this will play out long term!

Case Study: Author F

Genre: Omegaverse and reverse harem

Number of Books Published in English: 20 (some now unpublished)

Languages Translated Into: French, German, Italian, Dutch

Number of Books Translated (per language):

French – 11
German – 11
Dutch – 4
Italian – 4

Series or Standalones: Both; series, spin-off standalones, and standalone books within an interconnected world

Distribution Approach: Kindle Unlimited (except Dutch)

Advertising:

- Facebook Ads in French, German, and Italian
- French is the best-performing market
- No ads tried yet for Dutch (waiting for sales figures and expanding back catalogue)
- Previously spent $20/day on 5 ads; currently running two low-cost Facebook ads (totaling $6/day)

Proofreading/Quality Assurance:

ScribeShadow AI proofreading

Average Monthly Sales:

- April: $2,800 (10 books)
- May: $5,400 (25 books)
- June (projected, ads reduced to get a baseline): ~$3,800 (29 books, 4 Dutch in Kobo)
- Translation income is currently higher than English book income
- With ads running, daily income in France and Germany increased from ~$30/day to $150–200/day
- With only two low-cost ads, daily income is $100–$120 (including Dutch and Italian)

Author F kindly shared a screenshot of 3 months of their daily sales. Note: this does NOT include their Dutch wide sales!

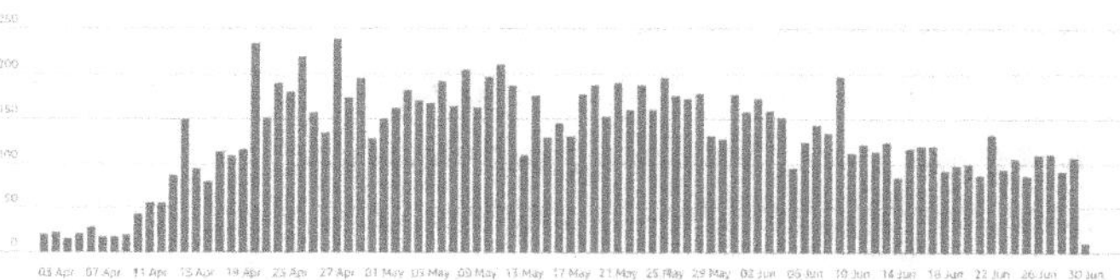

Surprises/Challenges:

- Surprised by the success of one particular series.
- French readers strongly prefer series over standalones
- Considering a new MF pen name to capitalize on French market demand for series

Workflow Tips & Advice:

- Start with one language and one pen name to leverage your back catalogue
- Translating all your books in one language helps maximize ad effectiveness and satisfies binge readers

Quote:

"Before I started translation on 6 April I earned approximately $30 a day in Germany and France, now I earn from $150 to $200 a day but only when I have FB ads running... Start with one language and one pen name to take advantage of your back catalogue, otherwise you'll need a lot of FB ads running to different markets and you won't be taking advantage of readers wanting to read everything you've written if you haven't translated it yet."

My analysis: This is another solid, steady performer with a good plan, building momentum (they are only 3 months in). It also bears out the fact that you sometimes really don't know which books and series are going to resonate in any given market, with one series surprising Author F in France.

Case Study: Author S

Genre: Historical Romance

Number of Books Published in English: 10 novellas

Languages Translated Into: German, French, Italian, Spanish, Brazilian Portuguese, Dutch

Number of Books Translated (per language): 6 in each language

Series or Standalones: Series

Distribution Approach: Kindle Unlimited (except Dutch)

Advertising:

- No ads currently
- Experimenting with Amazon ads for German, but results so far are negligible and not statistically significant

Proofreading/Quality Assurance:

ScribeShadow AI proofreading

Average Monthly Sales/Profit:

- Net profit (after paying ScribeShadow subscription costs) is currently negative (4 months in)
- German and French have covered their translation costs

Surprises/Challenges:

- Beware of the Dutch market! There is no Kindle Unlimited in the Netherlands, making it almost impossible to generate interest there via Amazon

Workflow Tips & Advice:

- When working with multiple languages, keep every detail organized in spreadsheets or tables; it's easy to get confused when you can't read the translations.

My analysis: Author S has expended a lot of effort, and quite a bit of money, translating these books into so many languages without any proof that they will sell. A good cautionary illustration as to why you should try to get things going in one language before moving on, even with a small ad spend. Nevertheless, my estimation is that this will eventually come good and get back into the black.

Remember, even your original books have setup expenses that they have to earn back!

Case Study: Author T

Genre: Crime/Mystery Fiction

Number of Books Published in English: 27 books in total. In crime/mystery/suspense: 16 (across 3 series; one more due out in August)

Languages Translated Into: German and French

Number of Books Translated (per language):
German – 7
French – 7

Series or Standalones: Series

Distribution Approach: Kindle Unlimited

Advertising:

- Facebook Ads in German and French
- Planning to try French/Canadian market soon

Proofreading/Quality Assurance:

- Used ProblemSolved for the first 6 German translations; now only using ScribeShadow with no additional proofing

Average Monthly Sales/Profit:

- France: Only just kicking off, about $50 per week profit post-ads
- Germany: Up and down, but around $50 per week profit at the moment (has been better in the past; needs ad tweaks)
- Not including increased English-language downloads from Germany & France in these figures, but they are noticeable

Surprises/Challenges:

- Was told German was the right market to start, but French seems better so far
- Surprised to see a similar number of negative reviews from both FR & DE, regardless of whether a paid human proofreader was used
- Considering how much more I paid for a "proofreader" from ProblemSolved, it's really concreted the idea of not bothering to use one

Workflow Tips & Advice:

- Main lesson: just get on and do it! Planning to

work on the next series as time permits

- Use DeepL to write ad copy because it's free and saves on ScribeShadow subscription
- Recommend going top level subscription on ScribeShadow to process translations quickly, then downgrading to save money when not actively translating

Quote:

"I think ScribeShadow might need a little more training (still working out how best to do that as each language is different) to get the best results, but with a very basic translation, I'm making a profit and seeing an increase in English version downloads from those countries, which I've not included in the profits."

My analysis: Another author seeing solid early results with a relatively conservative approach. Making sensible decisions based on analysis of results as they come in, Author T is setting up well for long-term success.

Final Words

If you've made it this far, congratulations. You're part of a new wave of indie authors who are not just dreaming about reaching readers around the world; you are actually going for it.

Translation, especially with the help of AI, is still a journey into the unknown. There is no one-size-fits-all formula. What worked for one author might not work for another, and success in one language or market does not guarantee the same in another, as the case studies amply demonstrate. But that is also what makes this moment so exciting: you are a pioneer, testing new waters and forging your own path.

As you have seen in these pages, some authors have found instant success in foreign markets. Others have faced unexpected challenges or slower starts. The common thread is that each tried, learned, adjusted, and kept going. The tools we have today are evolving fast, and so are the opportunities. Do not be afraid to experiment, and do not be discouraged by setbacks. Every step you take builds your experience and your reach.

Remember, you are not alone. The indie author community is vibrant and generous. Join groups, ask questions, share your wins and your struggles. Someone just starting out will be grateful for your advice, just as you were grateful for those who helped you.

Above all, never lose sight of why you started writing in the first place: to share your stories with readers. Now, with AI translation and a little courage, your stories can touch hearts and minds you never imagined.

So keep learning. Keep writing. Keep translating. The world is waiting for your words.

Here is to your next chapter, wherever and in whatever language it may be.

That's it.
Told you I didn't have anything to upsell you on.
Good luck!

Reference Checklist

Before You Translate

- Choose your strongest book or best-selling series as your first translation project. Choose ONE target language to start with, to prove the concept.
- Research your target language and market.
- Set your workflow. Determine if, and what type, of proofreading you will use, and recruit or book in if using human proofreaders.

Preparing Your Book

- Prepare your manuscript file (.docx or .epub) with simple formatting.
- Remove or set aside standard front and back matter (copyright, About the Author, etc.) to translate separately, as it only needs to be done

once.

- Translate titles, blurbs, keywords, and ad copy using ChatGPT or Claude.

Translation & Proofing

- After translation is complete, review the translation, chapter by chapter, for formatting errors or missing sections.
- Send off for human proofreading or beta reading in the target language, if that is part of your workflow.

Reformatting & Back Matter

- Reformat the final manuscript for ebook and print editions, adding in the translated copyright and About the Author pages.
- Update back matter with links, URLs, and newsletter signups for each language.
- Double-check interior layout for readability and accessibility.

Legal & Compliance

- Ensure your copyright page contains a contact name, postal address, and email, as required in the EU.
- Disclose AI use during the upload process, as required by Amazon or other platforms.

- Confirm you have the rights to translate and distribute your work.

Distribution & Pricing

- Decide where to sell for each translated language: KU or wide, and which platforms you'll upload to if you're going wide.
- Choose your primary marketplace and correct language/category settings on each platform.
- Set competitive prices for each marketplace.
- Consider paperback and special edition options, and research local distribution partners if needed.

Promotion & Tracking

- Set up or adapt country-specific ads (Facebook, Amazon, etc.) as budget allows.
- Maintain social media or outreach specific to your target markets.
- Track sales, KU reads, and ad performance by country and language.
- Tweak and experiment – international markets respond differently to covers, blurbs, and promotions.

Ongoing Maintenance

- Update back matter and links in all editions as

your catalogue grows.

- Stay informed: check for policy, tax, or royalty changes in your target markets.
- Join the ScribeShadow group on Facebook to keep up with trends and share experiences.
- When in doubt, ask for help! Indies are often generous with their knowledge and experience; there's a good chance someone else has already encountered (and solved) the problem you're facing.

www.ingramcontent.com/pod-product-compliance
Lightning Source LLC
Chambersburg PA
CBHW072239290326
41934CB00008BB/1350

* 9 7 8 1 9 2 3 1 9 5 1 6 5 *